BONHOEFFER

STUDY GUIDE

Also by Eric Metaxas

*Amazing Grace: William Wilberforce and
the Heroic Campaign to End Slavery*

Bonhoeffer: Pastor, Martyr, Prophet, Spy

Seven Men

FOUR SESSIONS

BONHOEFFER

The Life and Writings of Dietrich Bonhoeffer

ERIC METAXAS

WITH CHRISTINE M. ANDERSON

THOMAS NELSON
Since 1798

NASHVILLE DALLAS MEXICO CITY RIO DE JANEIRO

Published in Nashville, Tennessee, by Thomas Nelson. Thomas Nelson is a trademark of Thomas Nelson, Inc.

Thomas Nelson, Inc., titles may be purchased in bulk for educational, business, fund-raising, or sales promotional use. For information, please email SpecialMarkets@ThomasNelson.com.

Cover design: Kristen Vasgaard
Cover photo: ©Art Resource, NY
Interior design: Matthew Van Zomeren

ISBN 978-1-59555-588-5

Printed in the United States of America
14 15 16 17 18 QVS 9 8 7 6 5 4 3 2 1

CONTENTS

How to Use This Guide 7

SESSION 1
WHAT IS THE CHURCH? 9

SESSION 2
LIVING IN CHRISTIAN COMMUNITY 31

SESSION 3
RELIGIONLESS CHRISTIANITY 55

SESSION 4
COME AND DIE 79

Notes 99
About the Author 103

HOW TO USE THIS GUIDE

Group Size

The *Bonhoeffer* video study is designed to be experienced in a group setting such as a Bible study, Sunday school class, or any small group gathering. To ensure everyone has enough time to participate in discussions, it is recommended that large groups break up into smaller groups of four to six people each.

Materials Needed

Each participant should have his or her own study guide, which includes notes for video segments, directions for activities and discussion questions, as well as personal studies to deepen learning between sessions.

Timing

The time notations—for example (20 minutes)—indicate the *actual* time of video segments and the *suggested* times for each activity or discussion. For example:

✦ **Individual Activity: What I Want to Remember**
   (2 minutes)

Adhering to the suggested times will enable you to complete each session in 90 minutes. If you have only one hour for your meeting, you will need to use fewer questions for discussion. You may also opt to devote two meetings rather than one to each session. In addition to allowing discussions to be more spacious, this has the added advantage of allowing group members to read related chapters in the *Bonhoeffer* book and to complete the personal study between meetings. In the second meeting, devote the time allotted for watching the video to discussing group members' insights and questions from their reading and personal study.

Group Practice

Each session ends with a suggested application activity for group members to complete *together* between sessions. Although the activity is completed outside of the group meeting, it's a good idea to look over the group practice before concluding the meeting to clarify any questions and to make sure everyone is on board.

Facilitation

Each group should appoint a facilitator who is responsible for starting the video and for keeping track of time during discussions and activities. Facilitators may also read questions aloud and monitor discussions, prompting participants to respond and ensuring that everyone has the opportunity to participate.

Personal Studies

Maximize the impact of the curriculum with additional study between group sessions. Every personal study includes reflection questions on Bonhoeffer's life and teaching as well as a Bible study and a guided prayer activity. You'll get the most out of the study by setting aside about thirty minutes between sessions for personal study, as well as additional time to complete the group practice activities.

SESSION 1

WHAT IS THE CHURCH?

*The movement upward [toward God] cannot be separated
from the movement toward our neighbor. Both belong
indissolubly together ... Standing under God's rule means
living in community with God and with the church.*

DIETRICH BONHOEFFER, *SANCTORUM COMMUNIO*

✢ Welcome!

Welcome to Session 1 of *Bonhoeffer*. Each of the four sessions in this study is designed to be completed in 90 minutes. If you have only one hour for your meeting, you will need to choose fewer questions for your discussion. Your may also opt to devote two meetings rather than one to each session.

If this is your first time together as a group, take a moment to introduce yourselves to each other before watching the video. Then let's begin!

✢ Watch Video: What Is the Church? (20 minutes)

Play the video segment for Session 1. As you watch, use the outline provided to follow along or to take additional notes on anything that stands out to you.

NOTES

Dietrich Bonhoeffer was a pastor and a theologian. He had a passion for truth and a commitment to justice on behalf of those who face implacable evil.

Bonhoeffer was a member of the *Igel* (pronounced "eagle") fraternity at Tübingen University in 1923. *Igel* is the German word for hedgehog.

Karl Bonhoeffer wanted his children to think clearly — to follow rigorous logic to a conclusion and not be sidetracked by emotions. This was part of the Bonhoeffer family culture.

At eighteen, Bonhoeffer decided he wanted to spend a semester studying in Rome. There, he encountered a larger vision of the church:

> The universality of the church was illustrated in a marvelously effective manner. White, black, yellow members of religious orders—everyone was in clerical robes united under the church. It truly seems ideal.[1]

At twenty-one, Bonhoeffer completed his doctorate on the topic, "What is the church?"

At twenty-two, he spent a year in Barcelona, Spain, as the assistant vicar at a German-speaking church.

At twenty-four, he studied at Union Theological Seminary in New York City.

Bonhoeffer's cosmopolitan upbringing and the rigorous tradition of thinking clearly led him to think beyond national lines when it comes to the church.

Bonhoeffer's characteristics:

- He was not afraid to question things.
- He was always considering both sides of an issue.
- He was willing to think things through rigorously and never rejected anything out of hand.
- He was committed to a pure search for the truth. This meant asking, "What is God's idea of Germany?" Ultimately, this led him to reject Hitler and the political doctrine of the Nazi party called National Socialism.

What does this mean for us today?

1. *We have to consider Bonhoeffer's idea of a pure search for truth.*
   - We have to ask, "Am I just accepting tradition?"
   - What did the first-century church do? What did Jesus do? What are we to do?
   - We must have the confidence to be willing to question things.

2. *We need to take seriously the question, "What is the church?"*
   - Do we think along the lines of, "My church is the only real church"?
   - What does God say about the church? What are the non-negotiables for God?
   - You may have theological differences with someone, but does that put them outside God's church?

We ought to be challenged, and to think these things through without fear.

To confess and testify to the truth as it is in Jesus, and at the same time to love the enemies of that truth, his enemies and ours, and to love them with the infinite love of Jesus Christ, is indeed a narrow way. To believe the promise of Jesus that his followers shall possess the earth, and at the same time to face our enemies unarmed and defenseless, preferring to incur injustice rather than to do wrong ourselves, is indeed a narrow way ... If we regard this way as one we follow in obedience to an external command, if we are afraid of ourselves all the time, it is indeed an impossible way. But if we behold Jesus Christ going on before step by step, we shall not go astray.[2]

✛ Group Discussion (50 minutes)

Take time to talk about what you just watched.

1. What part of the teaching had the most impact on you?

THE CHURCH UNIVERSAL

2. Attending a mass in Rome, the eighteen-year-old Bonhoeffer witnessed an "ideal" picture of Christian community when he saw "white, black, yellow members of religious orders ... united under the church." Having been raised in a German Lutheran congregation, it was an experience that gave Bonhoeffer a much larger vision of the church.

• Why does it matter so much — for Bonhoeffer and for us — that the church is "universal"?

• What are the potential dangers when the definition of "church" is too closely associated with one culture or nationality?

• In what subtle or not-so-subtle ways do you think North American Christians today might be susceptible to blending cultural or national values into their understanding of the church?

3. Drawing on your own experiences, what vivid pictures come to mind when you think of the "ideal" church, or the church when it's at its best? For example, as with Bonhoeffer, it might be something you experienced in communal worship. Or it could also be something you experienced in relationship with someone, or something you witnessed in the world, etc.

What foundational truth or truths about the church are embodied in the experience you just described? In other words, based on your experience, how would you complete the following sentence: *The church is . . .*

4. Among the first pictures the Bible provides of the church—and one that Bonhoeffer relied on in describing his understanding of the church[3]—is the following passage from Acts 2. Go around the group and have a different person read each verse aloud. As the passage is read, underline any words or phrases that stand out to you.

> [42] All the believers devoted themselves to the apostles' teaching, and to fellowship, and to sharing in meals (including the Lord's Supper), and to prayer. [43] A deep sense of awe came over them all, and the apostles performed many miraculous signs and wonders. [44] And all the believers met together in one place and shared everything they had. [45] They sold their property and possessions and shared the money with those in need. [46] They worshiped together at the Temple each day, met in homes for the Lord's Supper, and shared their meals with great joy and generosity—[47] all the while praising God and enjoying the goodwill of all the people. And each day the Lord added to their fellowship those who were being saved. (Acts 2:42–47 NLT)

• What connections, if any, do you make between this description of the church and the personal experience you shared in response to question 3?

• At the mass in Rome, Bonhoeffer witnessed something beautiful he'd never experienced in church before. As you read the passage from Acts 2, what stood out most to you as something you've never experienced in church before but would like to? What is it about this expression of Christian community that you find especially compelling?

A PURE SEARCH FOR TRUTH

5. Bonhoeffer was not afraid to question things; he was willing to consider both sides of an issue and to think things through rigorously. Eric Metaxas described this as Bonhoeffer's willingness to engage in a "pure search for truth." In an emerging Nazi state, this search for truth led him to wrestle with the question, "What is God's idea of Germany?"

   • How do you feel about asking the question, "What is God's idea of my country?" In what ways might it be a productive question? In what ways might it be an unproductive question?

   • When it comes to the role of the church in the political sphere, we tend to err in one of two extremes: by either avoiding political issues altogether or by making political issues a litmus test of faith. How would you describe the dangers of both extremes? As part of your response, consider the potential impact of either approach on people both within and beyond the church.

6. Metaxas suggested that we have to be willing to question things in order to pursue the truth. For Bonhoeffer, this included not merely accepting the traditions and cultural expressions of the German Lutheran church he'd grown up in, but going back to the biblical texts and wrestling with the question, "What is the church?"

- How would you describe your comfort level when it comes to asking questions about the church that may not have easy answers?

- Based on your own church experiences, would you say the Christian community is open to questions and encourages thinking things through rigorously? Or does it tend to avoid exploring questions in favor of explaining answers?

GROUP LIFE

OPTIONAL GROUP DISCUSSION: THE MINISTRY OF LISTENING

Use this discussion if time permits, or if you are devoting two meetings to each session rather than one.

✢ ✢ ✢

An essential component of Bonhoeffer's life and legacy was his commitment to intentional Christian community, which he wrote about in his book, *Life Together*. Throughout this study, each session includes an optional discussion that is devoted to learning from Bonhoeffer specifically about Christian community, and to reflecting on your life together as a group.

(cont.)

In *Life Together,* Bonhoeffer devotes a chapter to describing various "ministries" that are to characterize authentic Christian community. Among them, he states that the first service we owe to others is the "ministry of listening."

> The beginning of love for the brethren is learning to listen to them ... Many people are looking for an ear that will listen. They do not find it among Christians, because these Christians are talking where they should be listening. But he who can no longer listen to his brother will soon no longer be listening to God either; he will be doing nothing but prattle in the presence of God too. This is the beginning of the death of the spiritual life ...
>
> Secular education today is aware that often a person can be helped merely by having someone who will listen to him seriously, and upon this insight it has constructed its own soul therapy, which has attracted great numbers of people, including Christians. But Christians have forgotten that the ministry of listening has been committed to them by him who is himself the great listener and whose work they should share. We should listen with the ears of God that we may speak the Word of God.[4]

- Briefly recall a time when someone listened to you in the way Bonhoeffer describes. Based on that experience, how would you describe what it means to "listen with the ears of God"?

- According to Bonhoeffer, listening is something we learn to do, which assumes some trial and error. If you were to somehow fail to listen well in this setting, how would you want the other members of the group to bring this to your attention *within the context of the group?* In other words, if it happens within the group, it needs to be addressed within the group—so how do you want the group to help you *learn* listening when you fail to listen well?

7. In addition to learning about Bonhoeffer together as a group, it's important to also be aware of how God is at work *among you*— especially in how you relate to each other and share your lives throughout the study. As you discuss the teaching in each session, there will be many opportunities to speak life-giving—and life-challenging—words, and to listen to one another deeply.

Take a few moments to consider the kinds of things that are important to you in this setting. As you anticipate the next few weeks of learning together in community, what do you need or want from the other members of the group? Use one or more of the sentence starters below, or your own statement, to help the group understand the best way to be a good companion to you throughout this study. As each person responds, use the two-page chart that follows to briefly note what is important to that person and how you can be a good companion to them.

It really helps me when ...
I tend to withdraw or feel anxious when ...
I'd like you to challenge me about ...
I'll know this group is a safe place if you ...
In our discussions, the best thing you could do for me is ...

Name	The Best Way I Can Be a Good Companion to This Person ...

Name	The Best Way I Can Be a Good Companion to This Person ...

✤ Individual Activity: What I Want to Remember
(2 minutes)

Complete this activity on your own.

1. Briefly review the outline and any notes you took.
2. In the space below, write down the most significant thing you gained in this session—from the teaching, activities, or discussions.

What I want to remember from this session . . .

NOTE: Each session in the *Bonhoeffer* study includes a group practice activity for group members to complete *together* between sessions. Although the activity is completed outside of the group meeting, it's a good idea to look over the group practice before concluding the meeting in order to coordinate plans or to clarify any questions group members may have.

GROUP PRACTICE: DISCOVERING A LARGER VISION OF THE CHURCH

Bonhoeffer's ideas about the church were challenged and shaped by his experiences in diverse settings and cultures—Rome, Barcelona, and New York City—as well as diverse worship styles (Roman Catholic, mainline Protestant, African American, etc.). Sometime during the duration of this study (and ideally within the next week or two), attend a church service together in your community where the worship style or cultural setting differs from that of your own church. Observe, listen, and talk to those you meet. Afterward, have coffee or share a meal together to talk about how worshiping with the larger Christian community both challenges and enriches your understanding of the church.

As an option, also consider learning more about how various churches—including your own—respond to the question, "What is the church?" Visit the websites for two or three diverse local churches (or visit denominational websites) and print out each one's statement of faith (sometimes simply called "what we believe"). Most statements of faith will include a section specifically about the church. Note the similarities and differences between what each statement says about the role and purpose of the church. Bring your observations and questions to the next group discussion.

✢ Closing Prayer

Close your time together with prayer.

SESSION 1 PERSONAL STUDY

✢ Read and Learn

Read the introduction and chapters 1 – 11 of the *Bonhoeffer* book. Use the space below to note any insights or questions you want to bring to the next group session.

✢ Study and Reflect

> To think of the church as something universal would change everything and would set in motion the entire course of Bonhoeffer's remaining life, because if the church was something that actually existed, then it existed not just in Germany or Rome, but beyond both. This glimpse of the church as something beyond the Lutheran Protestant Church of Germany, as a universal Christian community, was a revelation and an invitation to further thinking: *What is the church?*
>
> ERIC METAXAS, *BONHOEFFER*, PAGE 53

1. Bonhoeffer's ideas about the church were shaped by many factors, including his upbringing in the German Lutheran church, his mother's faith, his academic work in theology, and his experiences in diverse cultures and worship settings.

   Use the following list to briefly identify some of the factors that may have shaped your ideas about the church. Check the box next to any items that prompt a specific memory in you associated with church.

❑ Early childhood
❑ Young adulthood
❑ Parents
❑ Extended family members
❑ Teachers/mentors
❑ Pastor
❑ Student ministry leader
❑ Neighbors
❑ Colleagues
❑ Friends

❑ People at church
❑ Christian books and resources
❑ Christian media (television, radio, movies, digital)
❑ Church attendance
❑ Small group Bible studies
❑ Church scandals in the news
❑ International travel
❑ Church buildings
❑ Other: _____

2. Review the items you checked in question 1 and circle two: one that represents a positive memory and one that represents a negative memory. Briefly describe each memory below.

My positive memory related to church . . .

My negative memory related to church . . .

How have these experiences shaped your ideas about the church?

3. Bonhoeffer understood very clearly the failings of the church as well as its divine purpose:

> The church is a piece of the world; forsaken, godless, beneath the curse: vain, evil world—and that to the highest degree because she misuses the name of God, because in her God is made into a plaything, an idol. Indeed, she is an eternally forsaken and anti-Christian piece of the world in that she proudly removes herself from her solidarity with the evil world and lauds her own self. And yet: the church is a piece of qualified world, qualified through God's revealing, gracious Word, which she is obliged to deliver to the world which God has occupied and which he will never more set free. The church is the presence of God in the world. Really in the world, really the presence of God.[5]

In what ways do you recognize something of your own experiences and view of the church in Bonhoeffer's statement?

4. The New Testament writers use several metaphors to describe the church. For example:

- *A flock* (Luke 12:32; Acts 20:28; 1 Peter 5:2)
- *The body of Christ* (Romans 12:4–5; 1 Corinthians 12:27; Colossians 1:24)
- *The bride of Christ* (2 Corinthians 11:2; Ephesians 5:31–32; Revelation 19:7–8)
- *God's family* (2 Corinthians 6:18; Ephesians 2:19; 1 Timothy 5:1–2)
- *A spiritual house or temple* (Hebrews 3:6; 1 Peter 2:4–5; 1 Timothy 3:14–15)

Choose one or two of the metaphors that interest you and read the associated passages in your Bible. What do you find intriguing or insightful about this image of the church?

How does this image of the church challenge or affirm the experiences you wrote about in question 2?

5. Bonhoeffer believed that the church was Christ's presence on earth:

> Since the ascension, Christ's place on earth has been taken by his Body, the Church. The Church is the real presence of Christ. Once we have realized this truth we are well on the way to recovering an aspect of the Church's being which has been sadly neglected in the past. We should think of the Church not as an institution but as a *person*, though of course a person in a unique sense.[6]

Bonhoeffer specifically distinguishes between the institution of the church and the divine reality of the church in Christ. Drawing on your responses to questions 1 – 3 and what you've learned about Bonhoeffer's perspective, make two lists that state your own perspective about what the church is and is not. For example, "The church *is not* a building," "The church *is not* defined by race," "The church *is* made up of people who follow Christ," etc. Write down four to six statements under each heading.

The church is not . . .

The church is . . .

What do your statements reveal about what's important to you when it comes to the church?

6. In his book *Psalms*, Bonhoeffer writes about the presence of God in the church and what is required of God's people in response:

> What Mount Zion and the temple were for the Israelites the church of God throughout the world is for us—the church

where God always dwells with his people ... God has promised to be present in the worship of the congregation ... Christ brought in himself the sacrifice of God for us and our sacrifice for God. For us there remains only the sacrifice of praise and thanksgiving in prayers, hymns, and in a life lived according to God's commands (Psalms 15 and 50). So our entire life becomes worship, the offering of thanksgiving.[7]

Read Psalm 15, which describes the characteristics of those who dwell in God's sanctuary, the church. Drawing on the psalm as a reference, use the space below to write your own prayer. Acknowledge the questions you have about the church and ask for God's guidance. Invite God to help you with those things that keep you from making your "entire life worship." Thank him for his presence in your life and in the church.

BONHOEFFER STUDY GUIDE

✜ SESSION 2

LIVING IN CHRISTIAN COMMUNITY

The restoration of the church must surely depend on a new kind of monasticism, which has nothing in common with the old but a life of uncompromising discipleship, following Christ according to the Sermon on the Mount. I believe the time has come to gather people together to do this.

DIETRICH BONHOEFFER, LONDON, 1933–1935

✢ Group Discussion: Checking In (15 minutes)

A key part of getting to know God better is sharing your journey with others. Before watching the video, check in with each other about your experiences since the last session. For example:

- Briefly share your experience of the Session 1 group practice. What did you learn or experience when you visited another church, or researched the statements of faith from various churches?
- What insights did you discover in the personal study or in the chapters you read from the *Bonhoeffer* book?
- How did the last session impact your daily life or your relationship with God?
- What questions would you like to ask the other members of your group?

✢ Watch Video: Living in Christian Community
(23 minutes)

Play the video segment for Session 2. As you watch, use the outline provided to follow along or to take additional notes on anything that stands out to you.

NOTES

Finkenwalde was the site of the illegal seminary of the Confessing Church. There, Bonhoeffer attempted to create a Christian community where they would live by the principles of the Sermon on the Mount (Matthew 5–7).

Bonhoeffer's visit to the Abyssinian Baptist Church in Harlem changed his life. He had never seen Christianity like it. They were not merely *attending* church; they *were* the church. They were living out their faith. He later came to call this "religionless Christianity."

When I first started in theology, my idea of it was quite different—
rather more academic, probably. Now it has turned into something
else altogether. But I do believe that at last I am on the right track,
for the first time in my life. I often feel quite happy about it. I only
worry about being so afraid of what other people will think as to
get bogged down instead of going forward. I think I am right in
saying that I would only achieve true inner clarity and honesty by
really starting to take the Sermon on the Mount seriously.[8]

For Bonhoeffer, Christianity is less about intellectual insights and
theological observations and more about worship of Jesus Christ.
He wants to be an obedient disciple of Christ—that's number one.

It is ... high time for a final break with our theologically
grounded reserve about whatever is being done by the state—
which really only comes down to fear. "Speak out for those who
cannot speak"[9]—who in the church today still remembers that
this is the very least the Bible asks of us?[10]

Bonhoeffer felt the church had to be the conscience of the state.
This came to a flashpoint over the issue of the Jews. He says the
church is the place where Gentile and Jew stand together. God
looks on the heart, not at our bloodlines and last names.

The *Kirchenkampf* (church struggle) culminates in 1934 with the
writing of the Barmen Declaration, which declares a formal separa-
tion from the German *Reichskirche* (state church). The pastors who
sign it form what they call the "Confessing Church," to distinguish
themselves from the Nazified "German church."

Bonhoeffer wanted his Finkenwalde seminary students to live the principles of the Sermon on the Mount. He believed that real Christianity has as much to do with how we live as what we say we believe intellectually.

> Theological work and real pastoral fellowship can only grow in a life which is governed by gathering round the Word morning and evening and by fixed times of prayer.[11]
>
> A Christian fellowship lives and exists by the intercession of its members for one another, or it collapses. I can no longer condemn or hate a brother for whom I pray, no matter how much trouble he causes me. His face, that hitherto may have been strange and intolerable to me, is transformed in intercession into the countenance of a brother for whom Christ died, the face of a forgiven sinner.[12]

Mornings at Finkenwalde included: (1) observing silence after waking; (2) a 45-minute service that included singing hymns, reading passages from the Old and New Testaments and the Psalms, and prayer for the needs of the day; and (3) individual meditation on the Scripture of the day. Music was very important to Bonhoeffer. He also emphasized sports, games, and having fun. Bonhoeffer knew that living as a Christian has to do with the whole body, with being a human being, not just with the brain.

Bonhoeffer was trying to recreate New Testament Christianity. He wanted seminarians to know how to live as Christians in Christian community. He felt that living together—being Christians in community together—is another way we can worship God.

Bonhoeffer felt it was important for the ordinands to confess their sins one to another:

> Why is it that it is often easier for us to confess our sins to God than to a brother? God is holy and sinless, he is a just judge of evil and the enemy of all disobedience. But a brother is sinful as we are. He knows from his own experience the dark night of secret sin ... Our brother breaks the circle of self-deception. A man who confesses his sins in the presence of a brother knows that he is no longer alone with himself; he experiences the presence of God in the reality of the other person.[13]

Bonhoeffer felt it was important to have an atmosphere of joyful service.

One of the most important things that came out of Finkenwalde was the daily discipline of meditating on Scripture. It became a habit that sustained the seminarians and Bonhoeffer in the years to come.

We need to develop these spiritual disciplines now because we don't know what the future holds. We build these muscles now so we can use them later.

> Costly grace is the treasure hidden in the field; for the sake of it a man will gladly go and sell all that he has. It is the pearl of great price ... [for] which the merchant will sell all his goods. It is the kingly rule of Christ, for whose sake a man will pluck out the eye which causes him to stumble; it is the call of Jesus Christ at which the disciple leaves his nets and follows him.[14]

✣ Group Discussion (45 minutes)

Take time to talk about what you just watched.

1. What part of the teaching had the most impact on you?

CHURCH AND STATE

2. Bonhoeffer believed that the church must be the conscience of the state. This became a flashpoint over the issue of the Jews. In the first months of Nazi rule, churches were impacted when the Third Reich began executing its National Socialist agenda, which included a regulation called the Aryan Paragraph. Among other things, it mandated that government employees must be of Aryan descent. If the German church—essentially a state church—went along, all pastors with Jewish blood would be excluded from ministry. This violated the very nature of what Bonhoeffer and others understood to be the church, which made no such distinctions based on race (Galatians 3:28). In response, Bonhoeffer wrote his 1933 essay, "The Church and the Jewish Question." In it, he describes "three possible ways in which the church can act towards the state." Go around the group and have a different person read each of the three statements aloud.

> (1) [The church] can ask the state whether its actions are legitimate and in accordance with its character as state, i.e., it can throw the state back on its responsibilities.

> (2) It can aid the victims of state action. The church has an unconditional obligation to the victims of any ordering of society, even if they do not belong to the Christian community. "Do good to all people."

(3) The third possibility is not just to bandage the victims under the wheel, but to jam a spoke in the wheel itself [to stop the state from perpetrating evil]. Such action would be direct political action, and is only possible and desirable when the church sees the state fail in its function of creating law and order, i.e., when it sees the state unrestrainedly bring about too much or too little law and order. In both cases, it must see the existence of the state, and with it its own existence, threatened.[15]

- Do you agree or disagree with Bonhoeffer that the church should be the conscience of the state? Either way, what implications would your perspective have for how the church engages issues of justice?

- Overall, which of the three statements would you say best characterizes the way the North American church tends to engage the state (federal government) right now? Share any examples you can think of that illustrate your response.

- How would you describe the current "victims of state action" in your country? In other words, who tends to suffer because of laws and regulations (at the federal, state, and/or local level)?

- How would you describe your comfort level when it comes to engaging the government (federal, state, local) on the basis of your faith? For example, in advocating for reform on behalf of a marginalized or under-resourced group, addressing issues of corruption, or seeking to change laws or policies.

CHRISTIAN COMMUNITY

3. The pastors who signed the Barmen Declaration in 1934 formed what they called the "Confessing Church," to distinguish themselves from the Nazified "German church." They then commissioned Bonhoeffer to start a Confessing Church seminary. Bonhoeffer knew that Hitler and the Nazis could not be defeated with mere religion. He longed to see a church that had an intimate connection with Christ and was dedicated to hearing God's voice and obeying God's commands. But he knew this would never happen — that pastors couldn't hear, much less obey God — when prayer and meditating on the Scriptures were not even being taught in German seminaries. Neither were worship and singing taught. He determined that these would be the things he would teach in the seminary he was going to run. In a letter to his eldest brother, Karl-Friedrich, Bonhoeffer spoke about his decision to lead the seminary:

> The restoration of the church must surely depend on a new kind of monasticism, which has nothing in common with the old but a life of uncompromising discipleship, following Christ according to the Sermon on the Mount. I believe the time has come to gather people together and do this.[16]

- Traditionally, Christian monasticism is a withdrawal from society in order to devote oneself fully to Christ and spiritual work. Similarly, Finkenwalde was an experiment that took young ministers away from their routine lives for a time of full immersion in intentional Christian community. Why do you think Bonhoeffer considered it necessary to conduct his seminary this way?

- Bonhoeffer felt that what was especially missing from the life of Christians in Germany was the day-to-day reality of dying to self, of following Christ with every ounce of one's being in every moment, in every part of one's life. In what ways do you think sharing a communal life at Finkenwalde might have made dying to self and living for Christ both easier and harder for his students to practice?

4. Bonhoeffer's pursuit of "uncompromising discipleship" was grounded in his commitment to "following Christ according to the Sermon on the Mount." Jesus concludes his wide-ranging teachings in this famous sermon with a parable about wise and foolish builders:

> Everyone who hears these words of mine and puts them into practice is like a wise man who built his house on the rock. The rain came down, the streams rose, and the winds blew and beat against that house; yet it did not fall, because it had

its foundation on the rock. But everyone who hears these words of mine and does not put them into practice is like a foolish man who built his house on sand. The rain came down, the streams rose, and the winds blew and beat against that house, and it fell with a great crash. (Matthew 7:24–27)

• Based on what you've read and learned so far, what parallels do you recognize between the truths of this parable and the condition of the church in 1930s Germany? For example, consider the impact of Nazi ideology on the "German Christians" (aligned with the state church) versus those of the Confessing Church.

• How does the parable help you to understand Bonhoeffer's motives and strategy for how he chose to train his seminarians?

SPIRITUAL DISCIPLINES

5. Bonhoeffer was intent on training his students to hear God, which is part of the reason that each day at Finkenwalde began and ended with silence. He wanted the words of Scripture to be the last thing his students heard at night and the first thing they heard in the morning.

- What were the first words you heard or read this morning? To what degree did these words influence your outlook on the day ahead?

- How have you been trained to listen to God?

- What is your initial reaction to the idea of a daily practice of silence—of sitting quietly in God's presence and listening (without singing, reading, or saying anything)? For example, is it something you feel drawn to, or something you feel resistant to? Why?

6. Bonhoeffer insisted that his seminarians meditate on Scripture daily, seeking to hear what God had to say to them specifically for that day. It was a practice rooted in the belief that the Bible has the power not only to guide, present the gospel, and teach sound doctrine, but to routinely speak a personal word from God directly to each of us.

   - Overall, how would you describe your experiences of hearing from God through Scripture? For example, is it something you experience often or rarely? Do you tend to get a general impression or specific guidance? Are there experiences that stand out for any reason?

- Bonhoeffer's students found meditation on Scripture difficult and ceased to practice it for a period of time once while he was away traveling. These same students later realized how much this practice and other spiritual disciplines helped them in the terrible days of World War II. Why do you think so many of us resist practicing the disciplines that we know will strengthen us spiritually?

GROUP LIFE

OPTIONAL GROUP DISCUSSION: THE MINISTRY OF HELPFULNESS

Use this discussion if time permits, or if you are devoting two meetings to each session rather than one.

✛ ✛ ✛

After the ministry of listening (discussed at the end of Session 1), Bonhoeffer stated that the second service we must perform for others in Christian community is the "ministry of helpfulness."

This means, initially, simple assistance in trifling, external matters ... One who worries about the loss of time that such petty, outward acts of helpfulness entail is usually taking the importance of his own career too solemnly.

We must be ready to allow ourselves to be interrupted by God. God will be constantly crossing our paths and canceling our plans by sending us people with claims and petitions. We may pass them by, preoccupied with our more important tasks, as the priest passed by the man who had fallen among thieves, perhaps — reading the Bible. When we do that we pass by the visible sign of the Cross raised athwart our path to show us that, not our way, but God's way must be done ...

It is part of the discipline of humility that we must not spare our hand where it can perform a service and that we do not assume that our schedule is our own to manage, but allow it to be arranged by God.[17]

• Is active helpfulness something you expect from each other, or do you tend to think of this gathering primarily as a place for things like discussion, encouragement, and prayer?

• How comfortable would you feel asking this group for help with a practical matter? What factors contribute to or diminish your comfort level?

(cont.)

- What concerns you or intrigues you about the idea that your schedule is not your own to manage, but that you must allow it to be arranged by God?

7. At the end of the group discussion for Session 1, you had the opportunity to share what you need from the other members of the group and to write down the best ways you can be good companions to one another.

- Briefly restate what you asked for from the group in Session 1. What additions or clarifications would you like to make that would help the group know more about how to be a good companion to you? As each person responds, add any additional information to the Session 1 chart. (If you were absent from the last session, share your response to Session 1, question 7. Then use the chart to write down what is important to each member of the group.)

- In what ways, if any, did you find yourself responding differently to other members of the group in this session based on what they asked for in the previous session? What made that easy or difficult for you to do?

✢ Individual Activity: What I Want to Remember
(2 minutes)

Complete this activity on your own.

1. Briefly review the outline and any notes you took.
2. In the space below, write down the most significant thing you gained in this session—from the teaching, activities, or discussions.

What I want to remember from this session . . .

GROUP PRACTICE: READING SCRIPTURE IN COMMUNITY

Eric Metaxas stated that perhaps the most important thing that emerged from Bonhoeffer's experiment in Christian community at Finkenwalde was the daily discipline of reading and meditating on Scripture. Bonhoeffer and his students originally did this by gathering together for a service every morning, but it was also a practice they continued even after Finkenwalde closed and they were separated.

As a group, you can experience this aspect of Bonhoeffer's life and ministry by individually setting aside time each day to read the same Scripture passages. The suggested readings that follow are taken from the Book of Common Prayer Daily Office and include morning and evening psalms, as well as selections from the Old Testament, New

Testament epistles, and the Gospels. (Note that the Gospel readings begin with Matthew 5 and cover about half of the Sermon on the Mount, the foundational text for Bonhoeffer's life and for the Finkenwalde community.) If it will be more than one week between now and your next small group gathering, simply repeat the cycle of readings.

When you pray on your own each day, begin as Bonhoeffer and his students did, with a brief time of silence (one to five minutes). Ask the Lord to speak to you through what you read. Then read slowly and prayerfully, paying attention to any words or phrases that stand out to you.

After reading, spend time in silence again to listen for God, asking him to make his message clear to you. Close your time by praying for the other members of your group as well as for your own needs. You may also wish to make notes in a journal about your experience of reading and listening for God. You'll have a chance to discuss your experiences of reading and meditating on the same Scriptures at the beginning of the next group session.

Day 1
Morning Psalm: *Psalms 70–71*
Old Testament: *1 Kings 22:29–45*
Epistle: *1 Corinthians 2:14–3:15*
Gospel: *Matthew 5:1–10*
Evening Psalm: *Psalm 74*

Day 2
Morning Psalm: *Psalm 69*
Old Testament: *2 Kings 1:2–17*
Epistle: *1 Corinthians 3:16–23*
Gospel: *Matthew 5:11–16*
Evening Psalm: *Psalm 73*

Day 3
Morning Psalm: *Psalms 75–76*
Old Testament: *2 Kings 2:1–18*
Epistle: *1 Corinthians 4:1–7*
Gospel: *Matthew 5:17–20*
Evening Psalm: *Psalms 23, 27*

Day 4
Morning Psalm: *Psalm 80*
Old Testament: *2 Kings 5:1–19*
Epistle: *1 Corinthians 4:8–21*
Gospel: *Matthew 5:21–26*
Evening Psalm: *Psalms 77, 79*

Day 5
Morning Psalm: *Psalm 78:1–39*
Old Testament: *2 Kings 5:19–27*
Epistle: *1 Corinthians 5:1–8*
Gospel: *Matthew 5:27–37*
Evening Psalm: *Psalm 78:40–72*

Day 6
Morning Psalm: *Psalm 119:97–120*
Old Testament: *2 Kings 6:1–23*
Epistle: *1 Corinthians 5:9–6:8*
Gospel: *Matthew 5:38–48*
Evening Psalm: *Psalms 81–82*

Day 7
Morning Psalm: *Psalms 116–117*
Old Testament: *2 Kings 9:1–16*
Epistle: *1 Corinthians 6:12–20*
Gospel: *Matthew 6:1–6, 16–18*
Evening Psalm: *Psalms 85–86*

✢ Closing Prayer
Close your time together with prayer.

✣ Read and Learn

Read chapters 12 – 18 of the *Bonhoeffer* book. Use the space below to note any insights or questions you want to bring to the next group session.

✣ Study and Reflect

> I think I am right in saying that I would only achieve true inner clarity and honesty by really starting to take the Sermon on the Mount seriously.
>
> DIETRICH BONHOEFFER, *LONDON, 1933 – 1935*, PAGE 284

1. In a letter to Elizabeth Zinn, a woman to whom he had once been engaged, Bonhoeffer described how the Bible had led to a profound change in him:

> I plunged into work in a very unchristian way. An ... ambition that many noticed in me made my life difficult ... Then something happened, something that has changed and transformed my life to the present day. For the first time I discovered the Bible ... I had often preached. I had seen a great deal of the Church, and talked and preached about it — but I had not yet become a Christian ... Also I had never prayed, or prayed only very little ... Then the Bible, and in particular the Sermon on the Mount, freed me from that. Since then everything has changed. I have felt this plainly, and so have other people about me. It was a great liberation.[18]

Bonhoeffer's experience illustrates that it's possible to know a great deal about the Bible, to have spent a lot of time in church, and even to have preached the Bible, without "discovering" it.

Would you say that you have or have not discovered the Bible in the way Bonhoeffer describes? If so, what were the noticeable changes you experienced as a result? If not, how would you describe your relationship with the Bible right now? For example, does it bore you, frighten you, seem irrelevant?

2. When Bonhoeffer started the Confessing Church seminary at Finkenwalde, he was intent on training his students to hear and obey God through Scripture.

> I believe that the Bible alone is the answer to all our questions, and that we need only to ask repeatedly and a little humbly, in order to receive this answer. One cannot simply read the Bible, like other books. One must be prepared really to enquire of it. Only thus will it reveal itself. Only if we expect from it the ultimate answer, shall we receive it. That is because in the Bible God speaks to us. And one cannot simply think about God in one's own strength, one has to enquire of him. Only if we seek him will he answer us ... Only if we will venture to enter into the words of the Bible, as though in them this God were speaking to us who loves us and does not will to leave us ... along with our questions, only so shall we learn to rejoice in the Bible.[19]

Briefly identify a difficult relationship or a struggle you are facing right now. As part of your description, list any questions you have for God about this situation.

Bonhoeffer's statement about the Bible highlights several behaviors that characterize an authentic desire to hear God through Scripture. Use the following scale to assess the degree to which you recognize these behaviors in your efforts to hear from God about the difficulty you identified above.

3 = Completely true of me   1 = A little true of me
2 = Somewhat true of me   0 = Not true of me

_____   I have *repeatedly* sought to hear from God in Scripture.

_____   I have *humbly* sought to hear from God in Scripture.

_____   I have *expected* to hear from God in Scripture.

_____   I have *enquired* of God [asked God] to speak to me.

_____   I have *relied on* God and not attempted to think about God in my own strength.

_____   I have read Scripture as if God were *speaking directly to me.*

Choose one of the statements you rated lowest. What makes this particular action challenging for you?

3. The biblical text that changed Bonhoeffer's life, and the one he felt Christians should continually seek to live out, is the Sermon on the Mount (Matthew 5–7). Many of the specific teachings of the Sermon on the Mount are familiar, but it's also helpful to understand the scope of Jesus' teaching as a whole. For an overview of this foundational text, read the outline on the next page. As you read, underline any words or phrases that stand out to you.

What insights does looking at the Sermon on the Mount as a whole provide about what it means to follow Jesus?

Based on the outline, which passage(s) seem to relate most closely to the difficult situation you identified in question 2? Circle it on the outline and then look it up in your Bible.

Take a few moments to read the passage, following as best you can the guidelines Bonhoeffer described for seeking to hear from God. Use the space below to reflect on any connections you make between this Scripture and the difficulty you face.

THE SERMON ON THE MOUNT (MATTHEW 5 – 7)[20]

The Setting (5:1 – 2)

Introduction (5:3 – 16)

    Righteous Living: The Beatitudes (5:3 – 12)

    Discipleship: Salt and Light (5:13 – 16)

Main Body of the Sermon (5:17 – 6:34)

    The Relationship between the Old and the New Righteousness (5:17 – 48)

        Continuity with the Old Righteousness (5:17 – 20)

        Surpassing the Old Righteousness: Six Antitheses (5:21 – 48)

            On Murder, Anger, Disputes (5:21 – 26)

            On Adultery (5:27 – 30)

            On Divorce (5:31 – 32)

            On Oaths (5:33 – 37)

            On Retaliation and Dealing with Evil People (5:38 – 42)

            On Loving One's Enemies (5:43 – 48)

        Outward vs. Inward Righteousness (6:1 – 18)

            Giving to the Needy (6:1 – 4)

            Prayer and the Lord's Prayer (6:5 – 15)

                The Setting of Prayer (6:5 – 6)

                The Right Way to Pray (6:7 – 15)

            Fasting (6:16 – 18)

        Dependence on God (6:19 – 34)

            Serving God Rather than Wealth (6:19 – 24)

            The Disciple and Anxiety (6:25 – 34)

Various Teachings and the Golden Rule (7:1 – 12)

    On Not Judging Others (7:1 – 5)

    Discernment in Proclaiming the Gospel (7:6)

    The Answering Father: Ask, Seek, Knock (7:7 – 11)

    The Golden Rule (7:12)

Conclusion (7:13 – 27)

    The Narrow and Wide Gates (7:13 – 14)

    The True and the False (7:15 – 23)

        Warning against False Prophets (7:15 – 20)

        True and False Disciples (7:21 – 23)

    The Parable of the Wise and Foolish Builders (7:24 – 27)

The Astonishment of the Crowds (7:28 – 29)

4. Bonhoeffer made a direct connection between hearing from God through Scripture and obeying God:

> Humanly speaking, we could understand and interpret the Sermon on the Mount in a thousand different ways. Jesus knows only one possibility: simple surrender and obedience, not interpreting it or applying it, but doing and obeying it. That is the only way to hear his word. But again he does not mean that it is to be discussed as an ideal, he really means us to get on with it.[21]

> What is the "simple surrender" you sense God may be inviting you to in connection with the difficulty you face?

5. In his book *Psalms*, Bonhoeffer describes the grace and joy that come from knowing and following God's commands:

> Joy in the law and in the commands of God comes to us if God has given the great new direction to our life through Jesus Christ. That God could at one time conceal his command from me (Psalm 119:19), that he could allow me one day not to recognize his will, is the deepest anxiety of the new life.
>
> It is grace to know God's commands. They release us from self-made plans and conflicts. They make our steps certain and our way joyful. God gives his commands in order

that we may fulfill them, and "his commandments are not burdensome" (1 John 5:3) for him who has found all salvation in Jesus Christ.[22]

Read Psalm 119:17–32, which expresses the psalmist's desire to understand and follow God's commands. Use the psalm as the foundation for writing your own prayer in the space below. Acknowledge the challenges you face and ask God to reveal himself to you as you continue to seek him in Scripture. Ask him to help you experience the joy of being released from "self-made plans and conflicts." Thank him for speaking to you through his Word.

SESSION 3
RELIGIONLESS CHRISTIANITY

Who stands fast? Only the man whose final standard is
not his reason, his principles, his conscience, his freedom,
or his virtue, but who is ready to sacrifice all this when
he is called to obedient and responsible action in faith and
in exclusive allegiance to God — the responsible man,
who tries to make his whole life an answer to the question
and call of God.

DIETRICH BONHOEFFER, *LETTERS AND PAPERS FROM PRISON*

⊹ Group Discussion: Checking In (15 minutes)

A key part of getting to know God better is sharing your journey with others. Before watching the video, check in with each other about your experiences since the last session. For example:

- Briefly share your experience of the Session 2 group practice. What was it like to read and meditate on the daily Scriptures, knowing everyone was reading the same passages? In what ways did you find the practice meaningful or challenging?
- What insights did you discover in the personal study or in the chapters you read from the *Bonhoeffer* book?
- How did the last session impact your daily life or your relationship with God?
- What questions would you like to ask the other members of your group?

⊹ Watch Video: Religionless Christianity
(21 minutes)

Play the video segment for Session 3. As you watch, use the outline provided to follow along or to take additional notes on anything that stands out to you.

NOTES
Finkenwalde was officially shut down by the Gestapo in 1937. Eventually, the Nazis forbade Bonhoeffer from teaching, speaking publicly, and publishing.

The official German church had decided that their version of Christianity needed to be devoid of all Jewish elements.

Bonhoeffer was against the war that Hitler was bringing, which was a war of pure aggression and revenge for Germany's loss in World War I.

In June of 1939, Bonhoeffer sails for America. No sooner does he get on the ship than he begins to sense he may have made a mistake. Twenty-six days after he lands in New York, he sails back across the Atlantic to an unknown fate. He feels God is calling him to stand with his people in this great time of trial.

> Jesus Christ lived in the midst of his enemies. At the end all his disciples deserted him. On the Cross he was utterly alone, surrounded by evildoers and mockers. For this cause he had come, to bring peace to the enemies of God. So the Christian, too, belongs not in the seclusion of a cloistered life but in the thick of foes. There is his commission, his work.[23]

When Bonhoeffer comes home, he decides to officially become involved in the conspiracy by joining the Abwehr (German military intelligence). He is hired by his brother-in-law, Hans von Dohnanyi.

> Here and there people flee from public altercation into the sanctuary of private virtuousness. But anyone who does this must shut his mouth and his eyes to the injustice around him. Only at the cost of self-deception can he keep himself pure from the contamination arising from responsible action. In spite of all that he does, what he leaves undone will rob him of his peace of mind. He will either go to pieces because of this disquiet, or become the most hypocritical of Pharisees.[24]

Bonhoeffer met secretly with members of the allied governments. He wanted them to know there were Germans inside Germany working against Adolf Hitler. He was still working as a pastor, traveling, and writing his magnum opus, *Ethics*.

The big question: How does a pastor, a man of God, a faithful Christian, justify theologically the idea of getting involved in what becomes an assassination plot against the head of state?

It was becoming clear to him what it meant to live for God, to know God personally, to hear from God, and to try to do God's will in obedience.

The crux of the difference between what Bonhoeffer would call "dead religion" and actually being a faithful disciple of Jesus Christ is someone who is constantly saying, "Lord, wherever you lead me, I will go. Whatever you ask me to do, I will do."

> It is evident that the only appropriate conduct of men before God is the doing of his will. The Sermon on the Mount is there for the purpose of being done (Matthew 7:24ff). Only in doing can there be submission to the will of God ... When the Bible calls for action it does not refer a man to his own powers but to Jesus Christ himself. "Without me ye can do nothing" (John 15:5). This sentence is to be taken in its strictest sense. There is really no action without Jesus Christ.[25]

There is a difference between a negative religious faith—that says the whole point is to avoid sin—and a faith in the God of Scripture, a God who is for us, loves us, and desires for us to think of ourselves as his children. Bonhoeffer said that to obey God is more than trying to avoid committing a sin. He effectively said, I'm going to try to hear from God and do what he asks me to do, and even if I make a mistake, I serve a gracious God.

> Only in doing can there be submission to the will of God. In doing God's will man renounces every right and every justification of his own; he delivers himself humbly into the hands of the merciful Judge. If the Holy Scripture insists with such great urgency on doing, that is because it wishes to take away from man every possibility of self-justification before God on the basis of his own knowledge of good and evil. The Bible does not wish man's own deed to be set side by side with the deed of God, even as a thank-offering or sacrifice, but it sets man entirely within the action of God and subordinates human action to God's action. The error of the Pharisees, therefore, did not lie in their extremely strict insistence on the necessity for action, but rather in their failure to act. "They say, and do not do it."[26]

Bonhoeffer was very prayerful about becoming involved in the plot against Hitler, but he felt that he must act. He once said, "Silence in the face of evil is itself evil; God will not hold us guiltless. Not to speak is to speak. Not to act is to act."

> We have been silent witnesses of evil deeds; we have been drenched by many storms; we have learnt the arts of equivocation and pretense; experience has made us suspicious of others and kept us from being truthful and open ... Will our inward power of resistance be strong enough, and our honesty with ourselves remorseless enough, for us to find our way back to simplicity and straightforwardness?[27]

The Abwehr was the center of the conspiracy against Hitler. In April 1943, the Gestapo arrested Bonhoeffer for his involvement in *Unternehmen Sieben* ("Operation Seven") and took him to Tegel prison. Bonhoeffer's friend and confidante, Eberhard Bethge, buried Bonhoeffer's correspondence for safekeeping. These documents were later published as *Letters and Papers from Prison*.

By "religion" Bonhoeffer means *mere* religion. He means people who are not really obedient disciples, but are just going through the motions. Bonhoeffer believed the Nazis got the upper hand in Germany because the church had been merely religious. He felt what was needed was "religionless Christianity"—people who were being obedient disciples of Jesus Christ. In everything he did, Bonhoeffer tried to model this.

> I'm still discovering right up to this moment, that it is only by living completely in this world that one learns to have faith ... In so doing we throw ourselves completely into the arms of God, taking seriously not our own sufferings, but those of God in the world—watching with Christ in Gethsemane. How can success make us arrogant, or failure lead us astray, when we share in God's sufferings through a life of this kind? I'm glad to have been able to learn this, and I know I've been able to do so only along the road that I've travelled. So I'm grateful for the past and present, and content with them ... May God in his mercy lead us through these times; but above all, may he lead us to himself.[28]

✛ Group Discussion (45 minutes)

Take time to talk about what you just watched.

1. What part of the teaching had the most impact on you?

FOLLOWING GOD IN DIFFICULT PLACES

2. In June of 1939, Bonhoeffer left Germany for the safety of the United States. It was expected that he would stay for at least a year, but even as he was on the ship, he began to feel uneasy. Less than a month after his arrival, he returned to Germany. It was a decision that appeared to defy all logic and human wisdom. It also devastated his friends and colleagues, who considered it a miracle that he had been able to leave in the first place.

   • If you had been among his friends at the time, what arguments might you have used to convince Bonhoeffer that it was God's will for him to remain in the United States?

   • How do you relate to Bonhoeffer's decision? In other words, have you ever made a decision that appeared to defy all logic and human wisdom in order to pursue what you felt God was calling you to do? Briefly describe the situation, what made it risky, and what happened as a result.

- Among other things, Bonhoeffer experienced a persistent uneasiness that led him to wonder if he had missed God's intent and made a mistake in coming to the United States. In the personal decision you just described, what was it specifically that made you feel this was a decision God was calling you to make? Afterward, did you feel confirmed in the wisdom of your decision, or did you realize you had perhaps misunderstood what God was asking you to do?

OPTIONAL GROUP DISCUSSION: "IN THE THICK OF FOES"

Use this discussion if time permits, or if you are devoting two meetings to each session rather than one.

✛   ✛   ✛

Bonhoeffer's decision to return to Germany was a decision to live in the midst of enemies, which he considered in keeping with the example of Christ:

> Jesus Christ lived in the midst of his enemies. At the end all his disciples deserted him. On the Cross he was utterly alone, surrounded by evildoers and mockers. For this cause he had come, to bring peace to the enemies of God. So the Christian, too, belongs not in the seclusion of a cloistered life but in the thick of foes. There is his commission, his work.[29]

The threats Bonhoeffer faced from the Nazi regime are matched and even exceeded by those Christians face in many countries today. According to Open Doors, a nondenominational Christian ministry, 100 million Christians around the world currently suffer persecution. Examples of countries where persecution is considered extreme include North Korea, Saudi Arabia, Afghanistan, and Iraq.

- In light of Bonhoeffer's situation and the persecution faced by so many Christians around the world today, which of the following statements would you be more likely to agree with? Share the reasons for your choice.

  ❑ *Christians in North America may have challenges but, for the most part, they can't claim to have enemies.*
  ❑ *Christians in North America do have enemies, but they are rarely life threatening.*

- If a Christian from one of these countries were to tell you her story of persecution and then ask you who your enemies were, how would you respond?

- Bonhoeffer contrasted "the seclusion of cloistered life" with "living in the thick of foes." How would you describe these two realities within your Christian community? In other words, how do you and Christians you know tend to withdraw from or engage people and situations that are hostile to your faith?

OBEDIENCE IN ACTION

3. Bonhoeffer understood obedience as an active expression of allegiance to God:

> Who stands fast? Only the man whose final standard is not his reason, his principles, his conscience, his freedom, or his virtue, but who is ready to sacrifice all this when he is called to obedient and responsible action in faith and in exclusive allegiance to God—the responsible man, who tries to make his whole life an answer to the question and call of God.[30]

- Do you think it's possible to sincerely believe we have an exclusive allegiance to God, when what we really have is an allegiance to self—cloaked in reason, principles, conscience, freedom, or virtue?

- How do you imagine Bonhoeffer's decisions—about returning to Germany and becoming involved in the resistance—might have been different if they had been based on reason, principles, etc.?

- How does the distinction between human standards and exclusive allegiance to God shed light on the compromises and failures of the German church during this time?

• What are the potential dangers of trying to distinguish things such as reason and principles from allegiance to God?

4. Listed below are four verses highlighting various aspects of obedience. Go around the group and have a different person read each verse aloud. As the verses are read, underline any words or phrases that stand out to you.

> Jesus replied, "Anyone who loves me will obey my teaching ... Anyone who does not love me will not obey my teaching." (John 14:23–24)

> But Peter and the apostles replied, "We must obey God rather than any human authority." (Acts 5:29 NLT)

> By faith Abraham, when called to go to a place he would later receive as his inheritance, obeyed and went, even though he did not know where he was going. (Hebrews 11:8)

> Do not merely listen to the word, and so deceive yourselves. Do what it says. (James 1:22)

• Based on the passages you just read, what three to five words or phrases would you use to complete this sentence: *Biblical obedience is ...?*

- In what ways do you see, or fail to see, the characteristics you just described in Bonhoeffer's decision to return to Germany and in his actions in the conspiracy against Hitler?

5. Bonhoeffer was prayerful about his decision to become involved in the conspiracy against Hitler and believed he was being obedient to God's will when he did so. Based on what you've learned about Bonhoeffer's life and legacy, do you think this was genuinely what God was calling him to do? Or do you think he was sincere in his reasons but ultimately wrong in his decision? Share the reasons for your response.

"RELIGIONLESS CHRISTIANITY"

6. In a personal letter to his friend Eberhard Bethge, Bonhoeffer reflected on the failure of religion in Germany:

> The time when people could be told everything by means of words, whether theological or pious, is over, and so is the time of inwardness and conscience — and that means the time of religion in general. We are moving towards a completely religionless time; people as they are now simply cannot be religious any more. Even those who honestly describe themselves as "religious" do not in the least act up to it, and so they presumably mean something quite different by "religious."[31]

One of the characteristics of religion (or dead religion), in Bonhoeffer's view, was that it was passive and preoccupied with avoiding sin. In contrast, he believed that authentic faith ("religionless Christianity") was active and focused on hearing and doing the will of God.

How would you describe the difference in practical terms between a Christianity focused on sin avoidance and a Christianity focused on hearing and doing the will of God? Consider how the distinctions between the two might be evident in the actions of a church as well as those of individual Christians.

GROUP LIFE

OPTIONAL GROUP DISCUSSION: THE MINISTRY OF BEARING

Use this discussion if time permits, or if you are devoting two meetings to each session rather than one.

✢   ✢   ✢

In addition to the ministries of listening and helpfulness (discussed at the end of Sessions 1 and 2), Bonhoeffer stated that the third service we are called to perform for others in Christian community is the "ministry of bearing."

> "Bear ye one another's burdens, and so fulfill the law of Christ" (Galatians 6:2). Thus the law of Christ is a law of bearing. Bearing means forbearing and sustaining . . .
> The Christian . . . must bear the burden of a brother.

He must suffer and endure the brother. It is only when he is a burden that another person is really a brother and not merely an object to be manipulated.[32]

• Bonhoeffer describes bearing as both "forbearing and sustaining." To forbear is to be patient and tolerant, especially in connection with failure. To sustain is to nourish, and to provide emotional and moral support. What would you say are your strengths and weaknesses as a group when it comes to forbearing and sustaining?

Bonhoeffer continues:

The Bible speaks with remarkable frequency of "bearing." It is capable of expressing the whole work of Jesus Christ in this one word. "Surely he hath borne our griefs, and carried our sorrows ... the chastisement of our peace was upon him" (Isaiah 53:4–5). Therefore, the Bible can also characterize the whole life of the Christian as bearing the Cross. It is the fellowship of the Cross to experience the burden of the other. If one does not experience it, the fellowship he belongs to is not Christian ...

He who is bearing others knows that he himself is being borne, and only in this strength can he go on bearing.[33]

- Bonhoeffer makes a strong statement—that a community that fails to bear one another's burdens is not a Christian community. What implications does this have for Christians in North American culture, which tends to place a high value on independence and not wanting to be a burden?

- What risks would you have to take—as individuals and as a group—in order to grow stronger in the ministry of bearing?

7. Touch base with each other about how you're doing in the group. Use one of the sentence starters below, or your own statement, to help members of the group learn more about how to be good companions to you.

I want to give you permission to challenge me more about . . .
An area where I really need your help or sensitivity is . . .
It always helps me to feel more connected to the group when . . .
Something I've learned about myself because of this group is . . .

✛ Individual Activity: What I Want to Remember
(2 minutes)

Complete this activity on your own.

1. Briefly review the outline and any notes you took.
2. In the space below, write down the most significant thing you gained in this session — from the teaching, activities, or discussions.

What I want to remember from this session . . .

GROUP PRACTICE: HEARING AND DOING THE WILL OF GOD

This week, you'll continue the practice you began in Session 2 of setting aside time each day to read the same Scripture passages as a group, but this week you'll do so with an additional focus on responding in active obedience. (Note that the Gospel readings continue and complete the second half of the Sermon on the Mount, the foundational text for Bonhoeffer's life and for the Finkenwalde community). If it will be more than one week between now and your next gathering, simply repeat the cycle of readings.

As before, begin with a brief time of silence. Invite God to speak to you through what you read. Then read slowly and prayerfully, paying attention to any words or phrases that stand out to you.

After reading through the passages, choose one or two verses that caught your attention and read them again. As you read, reflect on these questions: *If I were to take these verses seriously, how would I respond? How might God be asking me to be obedient today?*

Take another moment of silence to listen for God, asking him to make his message clear to you. Close your time by praying for the other members of your group as well as for your own needs. Make notes on a pad of paper or in a journal about your experience of listening for God, and how you sense God is asking you to respond in obedience. You'll have a chance to discuss your experiences of meditating on Scripture and responding in obedience at the beginning of the next group session.

Day 1
Morning Psalm: *Psalm 88*
Old Testament: *2 Kings 9:17–37*
Epistle: *1 Corinthians 7:1–9*
Gospel: *Matthew 6:7–15*
Evening Psalm: *Psalms 91–92*

Day 2
Morning Psalm: *Psalms 87, 90*
Old Testament: *2 Kings 11:1–20a*
Epistle: *1 Corinthians 7:10–24*
Gospel: *Matthew 6:19–24*
Evening Psalm: *Psalm 136*

Day 3
Morning Psalm: *Psalm 89:1–18*
Old Testament: *2 Kings 17:24–41*
Epistle: *1 Corinthians 7:25–31*
Gospel: *Matthew 6:25–34*
Evening Psalm: *Psalm 89:19–52*

Day 4
Morning Psalm: *Psalms 97, 99*
Old Testament: *2 Chronicles 29:1–3, 30:1–27*
Epistle: *1 Corinthians 7:32–40*
Gospel: *Matthew 7:1–12*
Evening Psalm: *Psalms 94–95*

Day 5

Morning Psalm: *Psalms 101, 109*
Old Testament: 2 Kings 18:9—25
Epistle: *1 Corinthians 8:1—13*
Gospel: *Matthew 7:13—21*
Evening Psalm: *Psalm*
    119:121—144

Day 6

Morning Psalm: *Psalm 105:1—22*
Old Testament: 2 *Kings*
    18:28—37
Epistle: *1 Corinthians 9:1—15*
Gospel: *Matthew 7:22—29*
Evening Psalm: *Psalm*
    105:23—45

Day 7

Morning Psalm: *Psalm 102*
Old Testament: 2 *Kings 19:1—20*
Epistle: *1 Corinthians 9:16—27*
Gospel: *Matthew 8:1—17*
Evening Psalm: *Psalm 107:1—32*

✛ Closing Prayer

Close your time together with prayer.

GET A HEAD START ON THE DISCUSSION FOR SESSION 4

As part of the group discussion for Session 4, you'll have an opportunity to talk about what you've learned and experienced together throughout the *Bonhoeffer* study. Between now and your next meeting, consider taking a few moments to review the previous sessions and identify the teaching, discussions, or insights that stand out most to you. Use the worksheet on the following pages to briefly summarize the highlights of what you've learned and experienced.

SESSION 4 HEAD START WORKSHEET

Take a few moments to reflect on what you've learned and experienced throughout the *Bonhoeffer* study. You may want to review notes from the video teaching, what you wrote down for "What I Want to Remember" at the end of each group session, responses in the personal studies, etc. Here are some questions you might consider as part of your review:

- What insights did I gain from this session?
- What was the most important thing I learned about myself or my relationship with God in this session?
- How did I experience God's presence or leading related to this session?
- How did this session impact my relationships with the other people in the group?

Use the spaces provided below and on the next page to briefly summarize what you've learned and experienced for each session.

Session 1: *What Is the Church?*

Session 2: *Living in Christian Community*

Session 3: *Religionless Christianity*

✢ Read and Learn

Read chapters 19–27 of *Bonhoeffer*. Use the space below to note any insights or questions you want to bring to the next group session.

✢ Study and Reflect

> [Bonhoeffer] had theologically redefined the Christian life as something active, not reactive. It had nothing to do with avoiding sin or with merely talking or teaching or believing theological notions or principles or rules or tenets. It had everything to do with living one's whole life in obedience to God's call through action ... It was not a cramped, compromised, circumspect life, but a life lived in a kind of wild, joyful, full-throated freedom—that was what it was to obey God.
>
> ERIC METAXAS, *BONHOEFFER*, PAGE 446

1. Use the continuum below to assess how you tend to think about obedience in your relationship with God. Circle the number that best describes your response.

1	2	3	4	5	6	7	8	9	10

I think of obedience as avoiding sin and living a cramped, compromised, circumspect life.

I think of obedience as taking action and wild, joyful, full-throated freedom.

Briefly reflect on the last few days to identify a small way in which you acted in obedience to God. In what ways would you say that this experience of obedience was consistent or inconsistent with the number you circled on the continuum?

In recent weeks, how has your perspective on obedience influenced your relationship with God and your practice of faith? For example, in the way you pray, read Scripture, use your resources, worship, serve, etc.

2. The biblical writers repeatedly stress the importance of obedient action but they also affirm its joys and rewards, as with this passage from the book of James:

> Don't fool yourself into thinking that you are a listener when you are anything but, letting the Word go in one ear and out the other. Act on what you hear! Those who hear and don't act are like those who glance in the mirror, walk away, and two minutes later have no idea who they are, what they look like. But whoever catches a glimpse of the revealed counsel of God—the free life!—even out of the corner of his eye, and sticks with it, is no distracted scatterbrain but a man or woman of action. That person will find delight and affirmation in the action. (James 1:22–25 MSG)

Briefly identify one or two areas in which you are struggling to follow through on something you feel God is calling you to do. What accounts for your resistance?

What "delight and affirmation" would you hope to experience if you took the action God is calling you to take?

3. Bonhoeffer stressed an active faith and an obedient response to God's will not simply out of a gung-ho bias for action, but as a loving expression of allegiance to Christ:

> Only Christ himself can call us to follow him. But discipleship never consists in this or that specific action: it is always a decision, either for or against Jesus Christ.[34]

How does it impact your perspective on obedience to think of it not in terms of specific actions but as decisions made for or against Christ? Consider this especially in light of the areas of resistance you identified in question 2.

4. Read Psalm 119:57–64, which expresses the psalmist's desire to act swiftly on God's commands. Use the psalm as a reference for writing your own prayer in the space below. Confess the areas in which you are struggling with obedience. Ask for whatever it is you need in order to make a decision "for Christ" in those areas. Thank God for leading you in the way you should go.

SESSION 4
COME AND DIE

*I believe that God can and will bring good out of evil,
even out of the greatest evil. For that purpose he needs men
who make the best use of everything. I believe that God
will give us all the strength we need to help us to resist in
all time of distress. But he never gives it in advance, lest
we should rely on ourselves and not on him alone.*

DIETRICH BONHOEFFER, *LETTERS AND PAPERS FROM PRISON*

✚ Group Discussion: Checking In (15 minutes)

A key part of getting to know God better is sharing your journey with others. Before watching the video, briefly check in with each other about your experiences since the last session. For example:

- Briefly share your experience of the Session 3 group practice. In what ways did you sense God asking you to be obedient to the daily Scriptures? How did you respond?
- What insights did you discover in the personal study or in the chapters you read from the *Bonhoeffer* book?
- How did the last session impact your daily life or your relationship with God?
- What questions would you like to ask the other members of your group?

✚ Watch Video: Come and Die (23 minutes)

Play the video segment for Session 4. As you watch, use the outline provided to follow along or to take additional notes on anything that stands out to you.

NOTES

Bonhoeffer was brought to Tegel prison from his home in Charlottenburg in April 1943. He had been arrested for his involvement in *Unternehmen Sieben* ("Operation Seven"), an effort to get seven Jews out of Germany and into Switzerland.

In Tegel, Bonhoeffer often gave up some of his privileges because he knew that what was given to him would be taken away from other prisoners. He lived out his faith in small ways as well as large ways.

Bonhoeffer resolved that when he struggled with depression, he would stay in a good place mentally, spiritually, and emotionally as a means of being faithful to God. It took effort, but he had great reserves to draw on. He continued his daily spiritual disciplines in prison, meditating on Scripture and praying—for his family and for guidance from God. He wanted to hear from God: "Lord, what do you have to say to me today?"

We need to establish spiritual disciplines before we're in a place where we need them. We need to memorize Scripture.

Bonhoeffer ministered to others in prison—the sick, guards, prisoners. He functioned as a pastor in prison.

> I believe that nothing that happens to me is meaningless, and that it is good for us all that it should be so, even if it runs counter to our own wishes. As I see it, I'm here for some purpose, and I only hope I may fulfill it. In the light of the great purpose all our privations and disappointments are trivial ... If we survive during these coming weeks or months, we shall be able to see quite clearly that all has turned out for the best. The idea that we could have avoided many of life's difficulties if we had taken things more cautiously is too foolish to be entertained for a moment ... To renounce a full life and its real joys in order to avoid pain is neither Christian nor human.[35]

Bonhoeffer was given an opportunity to escape from Tegel prison. He decided not to because he felt the Nazis would be harder on his family if he did.

> I heard someone say yesterday that the last years had been completely wasted as far as he was concerned. I'm very glad that I have never yet had that feeling, even for a moment. Nor have I ever regretted my decision in the summer of 1939, for I'm firmly convinced—however strange it may seem—that my life has followed a straight and unbroken course, at any rate in its outward conduct. It has been an uninterrupted enrichment of experience, for which I can only be thankful. If I were to end my life here in these conditions, that would have a meaning that I think I could understand; on the other hand, everything might be a thorough preparation for a new start and a new task when peace comes.[36]

Bonhoeffer wrote many letters from prison.

Bonhoeffer and other high level prisoners were transferred to Buchenwald for several months near the end of the war.

> Why are we so afraid when we think about death?... Death is only dreadful for those who live in dread and fear of it. Death is not wild and terrible, if only we can be still and hold fast to God's Word. Death is not bitter, if we have not become bitter ourselves. Death is grace, the greatest gift of grace that God gives to people who believe in him.[37]

Bonhoeffer is taken to Flossenbürg concentration camp on April 8, 1945. On April 9, he is executed with a number of friends and coconspirators.

> Death reveals that the world is not as it should be but that it stands in need of redemption. Christ alone is the conquering of death.[38]

Bonhoeffer didn't fear death. He knew that Jesus had defeated death on the cross.

> No one has yet believed in God and the kingdom of God, no one has yet heard about the realm of the resurrected, and not been homesick from that hour, waiting and looking forward joyfully to being released from bodily existence.[39]

In *The Cost of Discipleship*, Bonhoeffer writes, "When Christ calls a man, he bids him come and die." He doesn't bid him come and clean up his act and try harder.

Bonhoeffer's whole life is a witness to that kind of thinking—that you have to know this to the point where you actually live it. It's God's will that we live it.

✛ Group Discussion (45 minutes)

Take a few minutes to talk about what you just watched.

1. What part of the teaching had the most impact on you?

FAITH IN PRISON

2. Bonhoeffer said that in order to bring good out of evil, God needs those "who make the best use of everything." He acted on this belief in a variety of ways while he was in prison.

   Drawing on what you've learned about Bonhoeffer as well as your own experiences, what do you think it means in practical terms to "make the best use of everything" in the midst of suffering? Consider this from various perspectives, such as physical, emotional, relational, spiritual, etc.

3. Viktor Frankl, an Austrian psychiatrist and Holocaust survivor, never met Bonhoeffer, but his description of exceptional fellow prisoners is one that might well have been written about Bonhoeffer:

   We who lived in concentration camps can remember the men who walked through the huts comforting others, giving away their last piece of bread. They may have been few in number, but they offer sufficient proof that everything can be taken from a man but one thing: the last of the human freedoms — to choose one's attitude in any given set of circumstances, to choose one's own way ... Fundamentally, therefore, any man can, even under such circumstances, decide what shall become of him—mentally and spiritually. He may retain his human dignity even in a concentration camp.[40]

- To suffer is to feel trapped by difficult circumstances we are powerless to change. In what ways, if any, do you think the suffering of the men who chose their attitude differed from that of the other men?

- As an act of faithfulness to God, Bonhoeffer determined that he would keep himself in a good place mentally, emotionally, and spiritually. When you are struggling, does it seem like you have a choice about how you respond—that you can actually determine to keep yourself in a good place? Or does it seem like your thoughts and emotions aren't things you have much of a choice about?

- Do you think it's possible to make the kind of choices made by Bonhoeffer and the men Frankl describes apart from faith in God? Why or why not?

SPIRITUAL RESERVES

4. Bonhoeffer drew strength from daily spiritual disciplines he had practiced for years before he was arrested, and that he continued to practice after his imprisonment. For example, he memorized and meditated on Scripture, sang hymns, and prayed for himself and others.

   • Eric Metaxas pointed out that we need to establish spiritual disciplines before we are in a place where we need them. In what ways do you imagine Bonhoeffer's experience might have been different if he had begun a daily practice of prayer and reading Scripture only after he was imprisoned?

   • How would you describe the level of your spiritual reserves right now—for example, are they on empty, half-full, full? If an unexpected crisis or tragedy were to happen, would it be more likely to weaken your faith and cause you to question God, or do you feel confident that your faith would be a source of strength you could rely on? Share the reasons for your response.

"COME AND DIE"

5. Bonhoeffer's views on discipleship are rooted in Jesus' teaching about the necessity of the cross:

   Whoever wants to be my disciple must deny themselves and take up their cross and follow me. For whoever wants to save their life will lose it, but whoever loses their life for me and for the gospel will save it. What good is it for someone to gain the whole world, yet forfeit their soul? (Mark 8:34–36)

In *The Cost of Discipleship*, Bonhoeffer writes:

> Discipleship means adherence to the person of Jesus, and therefore submission to the law of Christ which is the law of the cross ...
>
> To endure the cross is not a tragedy; it is the suffering which is the fruit of an exclusive allegiance to Jesus Christ. [It] is an essential part of the specifically Christian life ... If our Christianity has ceased to be serious about discipleship, if we have watered down the gospel into emotional uplift which makes no costly demands and which fails to distinguish between natural and Christian existence, then we cannot help regarding the cross as an ordinary everyday calamity, as one of the trials and tribulations of life ...
>
> The cross is not the terrible end to an otherwise godfearing and happy life, but it meets us at the beginning of our communion with Christ. When Christ calls a man, he bids him come and die.[41]

• Would you be more likely to say it was the series of events in Bonhoeffer's life that led him to this view of Christianity, or that his strong convictions about enduring the cross led to the events that unfolded in his life? Share the reasons for your response.

• What are some of the "costly demands" following Christ has made of you — in the past and recently?

- Have you tended to view these experiences of the cross as calamities, or were you able to see them as the natural outcome of your allegiance to Christ?

6. The camp doctor at Flossenbürg was H. Fischer-Hullstrüng. He had no idea whom he was watching at the time, but years later, he gave the following account of Bonhoeffer's last minutes alive:

> Through the half-open door in one room of the huts I saw Pastor Bonhoeffer, before taking off his prison garb, kneeling on the floor praying fervently to his God. I was most deeply moved by the way this unusually lovable man prayed, so devout and so certain that God heard his prayer. At the place of execution, he again said a short prayer and then climbed the steps to the gallows, brave and composed. His death ensued after a few seconds. In the almost fifty years that I worked as a doctor, I have hardly ever seen a man die so entirely submissive to the will of God.[42]

- How does this description of Bonhoeffer's death impact you?

- Years before his execution, Bonhoeffer preached a sermon in which he said: "Death is hell and night and cold, if it is not transformed by our faith. But that is just what is so marvelous, that we can transform death."[43] What do you think it means to die well, or to "transform death"? If you have known someone who died well, briefly describe the ways in which this person transformed death.

GROUP LIFE

OPTIONAL GROUP DISCUSSION: THE MINISTRY OF PROCLAIMING

Use this discussion if time permits, or if you are devoting two meetings to each session rather than one.

✝   ✝   ✝

As part of caring for one another within Christian community, Bonhoeffer prioritized the ministries of listening, helpfulness, and bearing (discussed at the end of Sessions 1, 2, and 3). Following these, Bonhoeffer identified the next service we are called to perform for others as the "ministry of proclaiming."

> What we are concerned with here is the free communication of the Word from person to person ... that unique situation in which one person bears witness in human words to another person, bespeaking the whole consolation of God, the admonition, the kindness, and the severity of God ...
>
> We speak to one another on the basis of the help we both need. We admonish one another to go the way that Christ bids us to go. We warn one another against the disobedience that is our common destruction. We are gentle and we are severe with one another, for we know both God's kindness and God's severity ...
>
> [God] has put his Word in our mouth. He wants it to be spoken through us.[44]

• To proclaim something is to state it emphatically or openly. Bonhoeffer names four ways we can proclaim the word of God to each other: in *consolation*, *admonition*, *kindness*, and *severity*. Overall, how would you describe the degree to which this group practices the ministry of proclaiming in each of these ways?

• Bonhoeffer acknowledged that there are "infinite perils" with the ministry of proclaiming, and stipulated that it must be preceded by the first three ministries—worthy listening, active helpfulness, and bearing/forbearing. Within this group, what concerns would you have about being a "proclaimer," someone who "bears witness in human words to another person" on behalf of God?

• No one likes the idea of being admonished or severely confronted, but is there anything that intrigues you about this aspect of the ministry of proclaiming? If someone in the group were to take the risk of admonishing or confronting you, how would you want them to do it?

7. Take a few moments to discuss what you've learned and experienced together throughout the *Bonhoeffer* study.

- How has learning more about Bonhoeffer's life deepened your understanding of the possibilities and significance of your own life?

- How have you recognized God at work in your life through the study?

- At the end of every session, you had an opportunity to talk about what you needed from the other members of the group and how you could be good companions for one another. What changes, if any, have you noticed in the ways you interact with each other now compared to the beginning of the study?

✛ Individual Activity: What I Want to Remember
(2 minutes)

Complete this activity on your own.

1. Briefly review the outline and any notes you took.
2. In the space below, write down the most significant thing you gained in this session—from the teaching, activities, or discussions.

What I want to remember from this session ...

GROUP PRACTICE: MEMORIZING SCRIPTURE

In addition to continuing the practice of setting aside time each day to read the same Scripture passages as a group, this week you'll also build up your spiritual reserves by memorizing a verse or two of Scripture. *You can do it!* Everyone chooses his or her own verses (unless the group is unanimous in wanting to memorize the same verses). You might choose to memorize a verse or passage that's already a favorite, or one you discovered recently through the daily readings. Potential options from the Sermon on the Mount include:

- One or more of the Beatitudes (Matthew 5:3–12)
- Salt and light (Matthew 5:13–16)
- Love for enemies (Matthew 5:43–45)
- The Lord's Prayer (Matthew 6:9–13)
- Do not worry (Matthew 6:25–26)
- Ask, seek, knock (Matthew 7:7–8)

Challenge and encourage each other, and celebrate your accomplishment soon by reciting your memorized verses for each other.

For your Scripture reading this week, continue as you have for the last two weeks by beginning with a brief time of silence. Invite God to speak to you through what you read. Then read slowly and prayerfully, paying attention to any words or phrases that stand out to you.

After reading, spend time in silence again, asking God to make his message clear to you. Close your time by praying for the other members of your group as well as for your own needs. Make notes on a pad of paper or in a journal about your experience of listening for God and how you sense God may be inviting you to respond.

Day 1
Morning Psalm: *Psalms 107:33−43, 108*
Old Testament: *2 Kings 19:21−36*
Epistle: *1 Corinthians 10:1−13*
Gospel: *Matthew 8:18−27*
Evening Psalm: *Psalm 33*

Day 2
Morning Psalm: *Psalm 106:1−18*
Old Testament: *2 Kings 21:1−18*
Epistle: *1 Corinthians 10:14−11:1*
Gospel: *Matthew 8:28−34*
Evening Psalm: *Psalm 106:19−48*

Day 3
Morning Psalm: *Psalms 120−123*
Old Testament: *2 Kings 22:1−13*
Epistle: *1 Corinthians 11:2, 17−22*
Gospel: *Matthew 9:1−8*
Evening Psalm: *Psalms 124−127*

Day 4
Morning Psalm: *Psalm 119:145−176*
Old Testament: *2 Kings 22:14−23:3*
Epistle: *1 Corinthians 11:23−34*
Gospel: *Matthew 9:9−17*
Evening Psalm: *Psalms 128−130*

Day 5

Morning Psalm: *Psalms 131–133*
Old Testament: *2 Kings*
   23:4–25
Epistle: *1 Corinthians 12:1–11*
Gospel: *Matthew 9:18–26*
Evening Psalm: *Psalms 134–135*

Day 6

Morning Psalm: *Psalms 140, 142*
Old Testament: *2 Kings*
   23:36–24:17
Epistle: *1 Corinthians 12:12–26*
Gospel: *Matthew 9:27–34*
Evening Psalm: *Psalms 141, 143*

Day 7

Morning Psalm: *Psalms 137, 144*
Old Testament: *Jeremiah*
   35:1–19
Epistle: *1 Corinthians 12:27–13:3*
Gospel: *Matthew 9:35–10:4*
Evening Psalm: *Psalm 104*

✛ Closing Prayer

Close your time together with prayer.

SESSION 4 PERSONAL STUDY

✛ Read and Learn

Read chapters 28–31 of *Bonhoeffer*. Use the space below to note any insights or questions you want to discuss sometime with a friend or group member.

✛ Study and Reflect

> The cross is the differential of the Christian religion, the power which enables the Christian to transcend the world and to win the victory.
>
> DIETRICH BONHOEFFER, *THE COST OF DISCIPLESHIP*, PAGE 153

1. In preparing the disciples for his impending death, Jesus said:

   > I am the good shepherd. The good shepherd sacrifices his life for the sheep ... The Father loves me because I sacrifice my life so I may take it back again. No one can take my life from me. I sacrifice it voluntarily. For I have the authority to lay it down when I want to and also to take it up again. For this is what my Father has commanded. (John 10:11, 17–18 NLT)

   Jesus states that his death is a choice—a sacrificial choice made from a position of power and authority. Why is it so important to make this distinction?

Jesus also called his followers to make the same sacrificial choice:

> If any of you wants to be my follower, you must turn from your selfish ways, take up your cross daily, and follow me. If you try to hang on to your life, you will lose it. But if you give up your life for my sake, you will save it. (Luke 9:23–24 NLT)

By Jesus' example and definition, a cross is only a cross when we choose it. How does this shape your understanding of what it means to take up your cross, and to do so daily?

2. Bonhoeffer acknowledged that because the cross is a choice, we have the option *not* to choose it — but even so, we bear a burden:

> We can of course shake off the burden which is laid upon us, but only find that we have a still heavier burden to carry — a yoke of our own choosing, the yoke of our self ... To go one's way under the sign of the cross is not misery and desperation, but peace and refreshment for the soul, it is the highest joy. Then we do not walk under our self-made laws and burdens, but under the yoke of him who knows us and who walks under the yoke with us. Under his yoke we are certain of his nearness and communion. It is he whom the disciple finds as he lifts up his cross.[45]

Recall a recent time in which you chose not to take up your cross (to deny yourself in some way). In what ways did you then experience the yoke of your own choosing, the yoke of yourself?

Bonhoeffer describes the experience of the cross with words like "peace," "refreshment," and "highest joy." Do you agree with Bonhoeffer's description? What three to five words or phrases would you use to describe your experiences of choosing to take up your cross in obedience to Christ?

3. In the routine choices to take up one's cross, Bonhoeffer recognized a kind of training ground or rehearsal for actual death:

> Those who live with Christ die daily to their own will. Christ in us gives us over to death so that he can live within us ... Christians receive their own death in this way, and in this way our physical death very truly becomes not the end but rather the fulfillment of our life with Jesus Christ.[46]

What connections do you make between this statement and the way Bonhoeffer faced his own death? (You may wish to reread Dr. H. Fischer-Hullstrüng's description of Bonhoeffer's death in the Session 4 group discussion.)

4. Bonhoeffer accepted death, but also affirmed that our hope in Christ is the promise of the resurrection:

> Death is, to be sure, the irrevocable bitter end for body and soul. It is the wages of sin, and the remembrance of it is necessary... On the other side of death, however, is the eternal God (Psalms 90 and 102). Therefore not death but life will triumph in the power of God ... We find this life in the resurrection of Jesus Christ and we ask for it in this life and in that to come.[47]

Read Psalm 90, a prayer of Moses, which describes the brevity of mortal life in light of God's everlasting faithfulness. Use the psalm as the foundation for writing your own prayer in the space below. Tell God about the places in your life where you are struggling to take up your cross. Ask him to give you the desire and the power to follow him. Thank him for his goodness to you—in this life and in the life to come.

NOTES

1. Dietrich Bonhoeffer, *The Young Bonhoeffer: 1918–1927*, Dietrich Bonhoeffer Works, vol. 9, Wayne Whitson Floyd Jr., gen. ed. (Minneapolis: Augsburg Fortress, 2003), 88.

2. Dietrich Bonhoeffer, *The Cost of Discipleship* (New York: Simon and Schuster, 1995), 190.

3. Dietrich Bonhoeffer, "The Visible Church in the New Testament," reproduced in *A Testament to Freedom*, Geffrey B. Kelly and F. Burton Nelson, eds. (San Francisco: HarperSanFrancisco, 1990, 1995), 155.

4. Dietrich Bonhoeffer, *Life Together: The Classic Exploration of Christian Community* (New York: Harper and Row 1954), 97, 98–99.

5. Dietrich Bonhoeffer, quoted in John A. Phillips, *The Form of Christ in the World: A Study of Bonhoeffer's Christology* (London: Collins, 1967), 113.

6. Bonhoeffer, *The Cost of Discipleship*, 241.

7. Dietrich Bonhoeffer, *Psalms: The Prayer Book of the Bible* (Minneapolis: Augsburg Fortress, 1970), 40, 41.

8. Dietrich Bonhoeffer, in a letter to his eldest brother, Karl-Friedrich, *London, 1933–1935*, Dietrich Bonhoeffer Works, vol. 13 (Minneapolis: Augsburg Fortress, 2007), 284.

9. Proverbs 31:8.

10. Dietrich Bonhoeffer, in a letter to his Swiss friend Erwin

Sutz, with whom he had been a student at Union Seminary, *London, 1933–1935*, 17.

11. Letter to friend and theologian Karl Barth, quoted in *A Testament to Freedom: The Essential Writings of Dietrich Bonhoeffer*, Geffrey B. Kelly and F. Burton Nelson, eds. (San Francisco: HarperSanFrancisco, 1990, 1995), 431.

12. Bonhoeffer, *Life Together*, 86.

13. Bonhoeffer, *Life Together*, 115, 116.

14. Bonhoeffer, *The Cost of Discipleship*, 45.

15. Dietrich Bonhoeffer, *No Rusty Swords: Letters, Lectures and Notes 1928–1936* (New York: Harper and Row 1965), 225.

16. Bonhoeffer, *London, 1933–1935*, 284.

17. Bonhoeffer, *Life Together*, 99.

18. Bonhoeffer, *A Testament to Freedom*, 424–425.

19. Mary Bosanquet, *The Life and Death of Dietrich Bonhoeffer* (New York: Harper and Row, 1968), 109.

20. Adapted from Donald A. Hagner, *Matthew 1–13*, Word Biblical Commentary, vol. 33A, Ralph P. Martin, ed. (Dallas: Word Books, 1993), vii-viii.

21. Bonhoeffer, *The Cost of Discipleship*, 196–197.

22. Bonhoeffer, *Psalms*, 31–32.

23. Bonhoeffer, *Life Together*, 17.

24. Bonhoeffer, *Letters and Papers from Prison*, 5.

25. Dietrich Bonhoeffer, *Ethics* (New York: Touchstone, 1995), 46.

26. Bonhoeffer, *Ethics*, 46.

27. Bonhoeffer, *Letters and Papers from Prison*, 16, 17.

28. Bonhoeffer, *Letters and Papers from Prison*, 369, 370.

29. Bonhoeffer, *Life Together*, 17.

30. Bonhoeffer, *Letters and Papers from Prison*, 5.

31. Bonhoeffer, *Letters and Papers from Prison*, 279.

32 Bonhoeffer, *Life Together*, 100.

33. Bonhoeffer, *Life Together*, 101, 103.

34. Bonhoeffer, *The Cost of Discipleship*, 226.

35. Bonhoeffer, *Letters and Papers from Prison*, 289, 191.

36. Bonhoeffer, *Letters and Papers from Prison*, 272.

37. Bonhoeffer, *London, 1933–1935*, 331, 335.

38. Dietrich Bonhoeffer, *Conspiracy and Imprisonment, 1940–1945*, Dietrich Bonhoeffer Works, vol. 16, Mark S. Brocker, ed. (Minneapolis: Fortress Press, 2006), 207.

39. Bonhoeffer, *London: 1933–1935*, 334.

40. Viktor E. Frankl, *Man's Search for Meaning* (Boston: Beacon Press, 1959, 1962, 1984, 1992), 75.

41. Bonhoeffer, *The Cost of Discipleship*, 87, 88–89.

42. Eberhard Bethge, *Dietrich Bonhoeffer: A Biography* (Minneapolis: Fortress Press, 2000), 927–928.

43. Bonhoeffer, *London: 1933–1935*, 335.

44. Bonhoeffer, *Life Together*, 103–104, 106, 108.

45. Bonhoeffer, *The Cost of Discipleship*, 92–93.

46. Bonhoeffer, *Conspiracy and Imprisonment*, 208.

47. Bonhoeffer, *Psalms*, 62.

ABOUT THE AUTHOR

Eric Metaxas is the author of the *New York Times* number-one bestseller and ECPA "Book of the Year" *Bonhoeffer: Pastor, Martyr, Prophet, Spy*, the bestseller *Amazing Grace: William Wilberforce and the Heroic Campaign to End Slavery*, and more than thirty other books. His most recent book, titled *Seven Men*, explores the secrets of greatness of Bonhoeffer, Wilberforce, and five others, including George Washington, Eric Liddell, and Jackie Robinson.

Metaxas is currently the voice of *BreakPoint*, a radio commentary broadcast on fourteen hundred radio outlets with an audience of 8 million. He was the keynote speaker at the 2012 National Prayer Breakfast in Washington, DC, and was awarded the Canterbury Medal in 2011 by the Becket Fund for Religious Freedom. Metaxas has written for VeggieTales, Chuck Colson, and the *New York Times*. He lives in New York with his wife and daughter.

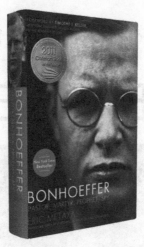

"BONHOEFFER IS THE STORY OF A LIFE
framed by a passion for truth and a commitment to justice on behalf
of those who face implacable evil. [A] beautifully constructed
biography." ALAN WOLFE, *The New Republic* • "Metaxas tells
Bonhoeffer's story with passion and theological sophistication...."
WALL STREET JOURNAL • "[A] weighty, riveting analysis of the
life of Dietrich Bonhoeffer...." *PUBLISHERS WEEKLY* • "Metaxas
presents Bonhoeffer as a clear-headed, deeply convicted Christian
who submitted to no one and nothing except God and his Word."
CHRISTIANITY TODAY • "Metaxas has written a book that
adds a new dimension to World War II, a new understanding
of how evil can seize the soul of a nation and a man of faith can
confront it...." THOMAS FLEMING, *author, The New Dealers'
War* • "Metaxas has created a biography of uncommon power—
intelligent, moving, well researched, vividly written, and
rich in implication for our own lives. Or to put it another way: Buy this book. Read it. Then buy another copy
and give it to a person you love. It's that good." ARCHBISHOP
CHARLES CHAPUT, *First Things* • "A definitive Bonhoeffer
biography for the 21st century." *KIRKUS REVIEWS*

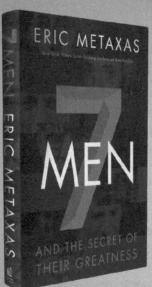

Tools for Your Church or Small Group

You'll Get Through This DVD
978-0-8499-5997-4 | $26.99

Max Lucado leads six video sessions, which will help small group participants apply the truth of Genesis 50:20 to their own lives. What Satan intends for evil, God redeems for good.

You'll Get Through This
Study Guide
978-0-8499-5998-1 | $10.99

Filled with Scripture study, discussion questions, and practical ideas designed to lead group members through the story of Joseph and remind us all to trust God to trump evil, this guide is an integral part of the *You'll Get Through This* small group study.

God Will Use This for Good
978-0-8499-4754-4 | $2.99

Featuring key selections from *You'll Get Through This*, scripture promises, and a gospel presentation, this 64-page booklet is ideal for passing along to friends who are facing turbulent times.

Fight

Winning the Battles That Matter Most

Craig Groeschel

Author and pastor Craig Groeschel helps you uncover who you really are — a man created in the image of God with a warrior's heart — and how to fight the good fight for what's right. You will find the strength to fight the battles you know you need to fight — the ones that determine the state of your heart, the quality of your marriage, and the spiritual health of your family.

Craig will also look at examples from the Bible, including our good buddy Samson. Yep, the dude with the rippling biceps, hippie hair, and a thing for Delilah. You may be surprised how much we have in common with this guy. By looking at his life, you'll learn how to defeat the demons that make strong men weak. You'll become who God made you to be:

A man who knows how to fight for what's right.

And don't you dare show up for this fight unarmed. Learn how to fight with faith, with prayer, and with the Word of God

It's time to fight like a man. For God's Sake, FIGHT.

Available in stores and online!